Pebble® Plus

Plant Parts
Roots

by Vijaya Khisty Bodach

Consulting Editor: Gail Saunders-Smith, PhD

Consultant: Judson R. Scott, Current President
American Society of Consulting Arborists

Capstone
press®

Mankato, Minnesota

Pebble Plus is published by Capstone Press,
151 Good Counsel Drive, P.O. Box 669, Mankato, Minnesota 56002.
www.capstonepress.com

1 2 3 4 5 6 11 10 09 08 07 06

Library of Congress Cataloging-in-Publication Data
Bodach, Vijaya Khisty.
　　Roots / by Vijaya Khisty Bodach.
　　p. cm.—(Pebble plus. Plant parts)
　　Summary: "Simple text and photographs present the roots of plants, how they grow, and their
uses"—Provided by publisher.
　　Includes bibliographical references and index.
　　ISBN-13: 978-0-7368-6345-2 (hardcover)
　　ISBN-10: 0-7368-6345-1 (hardcover)
　　ISBN-13: 978-0-7368-7546-2 (softcover pbk.)
　　ISBN-10: 0-7368-7546-8 (softcover pbk.)
　　1. Roots (Botany)—Juvenile literature. I. Title. II. Series.
QK644.B62 2007
575.5'4—dc22   2006000993

Editorial Credits
Sarah L. Schuette, editor; Jennifer Bergstrom, designer; Kelly Garvin, photo researcher/photo editor

Photo Credits
Capstone Press/Karon Dubke, cover, 1
Dwight R. Kuhn, 7, 16–17, 20–21, 22 (all)
Peter Arnold/Luiz C. Marigo, 4–5; Roland Birke, 9
Shutterstock/Adrian T. Jones, 10–11; Jim Parkin, 12–13; Tihis, 14–15
Visuals Unlimited/David Cavagnaro, 18–19

Note to Parents and Teachers

The Plant Parts set supports national science standards related to identifying plant parts
and the diversity and interdependence of life. This book describes and illustrates roots.
The images support early readers in understanding the text. The repetition of words and
phrases helps early readers learn new words. This book also introduces early readers
to subject-specific vocabulary words, which are defined in the Glossary section. Early
readers may need assistance to read some words and to use the Table of Contents,
Glossary, Read More, Internet Sites, and Index sections of the book.

Table of Contents

Plants Need Roots 4

All Kinds of Roots 10

Roots We Eat 16

Wonderful Roots 20

Parts of a Corn Plant 22

Glossary 23

Read More 23

Index 24

Internet Sites 24

Plants Need Roots

Roots keep plants
from falling over.
Roots grow down
into the ground.

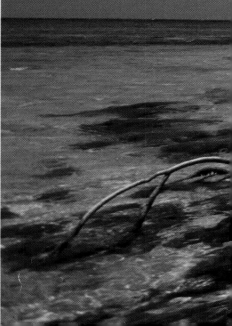

Roots get food
for the whole plant.
They suck up food
and water from the soil.

Roots send food
up plant stems.
Stems carry the food
to the rest of the plant.

9

All Kinds of Roots

Long tree roots spread out
under the soil.

They search for water below.

Shallow cactus roots

soak up rain quickly.

They store water

for the plant.

Water lily roots
grow down into the mud.
Roots keep the plants
from floating away.

Roots We Eat

We eat some roots.

Carrots are the tap roots

of green leafy carrot plants.

Turnips are root vegetables.
They taste good in soups
and salads.

Wonderful Roots

Deep or shallow,

thick or thin,

roots help plants

stay alive.

Parts of a Corn Plant

seed

stem

roots

leaves

Glossary

soil—the dirt where plants grow; most plants get their food and water from the soil.

stem—the long main part of a plant that makes leaves; food gathered by roots moves through stems to the rest of the plant.

tap root—a long, thick plant part that grows into the ground; carrots are tap roots.

Read More

Blackaby, Susan. *Plant Plumbing: A Book About Roots and Stems.* Growing Things. Minneapolis: Picture Window Books, 2003.

Farndon, John. *Roots.* World of Plants. San Diego: Blackbirch Press, 2005.

Kudlinski, Kathleen V. *What Do Roots Do?* Minnetonka, Minn.: NorthWord Books, 2005.

Index

cactus, 12

carrots, 16

food, 6, 8

rain, 12

soil, 6, 10

stems, 8

tap roots, 16

turnips, 18

water, 6, 10, 12

water lily, 14

Word Count: 121
Grade: 1
Early-Intervention Level: 15

Internet Sites

FactHound offers a safe, fun way to find Internet sites related to this book. All of the sites on FactHound have been researched by our staff.

Here's how:

1. Visit *www.facthound.com*

2. Choose your grade level.

3. Type in this book ID **0736863451** for age-appropriate sites. You may also browse subjects by clicking on letters, or by clicking on pictures and words.

4. Click on the **Fetch It** button.

Facthound will fetch the best sites for you!